in memory of
Catherine Deane,
and her two sons
James and Anthony

# An Urgency of Stars

Geraldine Mills

ARLEN
HOUSE

Published in 2010 by
ARLEN HOUSE
*an imprint of Arlen Publications Ltd*
PO Box 222
Galway
Phone/Fax: 353 86 8207617
Email: arlenhouse@gmail.com


Distributed Internationally by
SYRACUSE UNIVERSITY PRESS
621 Skytop Road, Suite 110
Syracuse, NY 13244–5290
Phone: 315–443–5534/Fax: 315–443–5545
Email: supress@syr.edu


ISBN 978–0–905223–53–7, paperback
ISBN 978–0–905223–60–5, hardback
*(a signed and numbered limited edition is also available)*

Cover Artwork
front: Charlotte Kelly, 'Taking Flight', *oil on canvas*
back: Charlotte Kelly, 'The Crossing', *oil on canvas*
reproduced courtesy of the artist

Typesetting by Arlen House
Printed in Ireland

# CONTENTS

## THESE ARE THE ONLY JOURNEYS

That winter had one month too many.
Each day brought storms that plundered,
the window panes iced over,
the cold came too close.

It was the season when our children left
to slip into their own skins.
If they stayed, they died.
There are no other journeys.

With no shelter to hide behind,
there was cold enough for both of us.
Like seals, all we could do was
breathe holes in the ice to survive.

## CHANGING GROUND

I have spoken to no one for days
but the small bird with the black band
of neck as it bobs its way in front of me;
it feigns nesting in the torc of wrack in the sand.

A man in a scrapie wool jumper
picks broken teeth from the strand;
if he opens the black cavern of his mouth
and utters three, two, even one word,
I'll be gone with him.

The day comes when you can no longer
squeeze into the old coat of yourself.

Slievemore stays where it is,
never moved its whole old life.
It waits for the farmers to shift
their animals up and down with the seasons.

My bones know change the way birds know sky,
the way they let go of light over the deserted village,
the way the grass knows it, bitten down to the quick.

We were able to find our way once.
Geographers sailed from Cádiz to Galway,
then on to new places in the New World.
Emigrants caught mail boats and cut their way
through jungles of strangers' faces to search out
the liquids and mutes of their own tongue
in the pubs of Cricklewood or the Bronx.
Even those who believed that feet grew out
of peoples' heads south of the Equator
still managed to navigate oceans,
steering by sun and stars,
on silken routes that trapped the monsoon winds.

Now we know that if we dig our way
through the earth's core we will emerge
like prairie dogs at our antipodes:
Auckland at Seville, Fiji at Timbuktu,
Bermuda at Perth.
Never so many signposts, and never so hopelessly lost.
An extra limb attached to our ears, we spend our time
searching throughout the supermarket, city, street,
calling, texting, calling, *tell me where you are?*
But we give no answer, afraid to dig a way
into the core of our selves, because we have
no internal sat nav to talk us back.

FRANCIS BACON DREAMS A SUBURBAN WIFE

Suddenly dusk, she climbs the rope ladder
up into his studio, closes the window on sounds
rising from the evening street, gathers up brushes,
frayed ends of sleeves, corduroy swatches.
She sorts his piles of newspaper cuttings,
slips them into clear plastic pockets,
alphabetical, chronological,
puts torn leaves of books back in their place.
She releases the chairs and cupboard
that she winched to the ceiling that morning
to allow him more space, switches off the light.

Downstairs she admires the new name
from Tudor Close in the visitor's book
before she enters the room to pour his gin,
hurries the children to sleep
and returns to effleurage his back, stiff
from painting a cottage scene in the west,
all window boxes and tea roses
occluding the doorway.

Saturdays, she lets him take flight
with a white ball down a straight fairway,
his polo shirt nicely pressed, gloves on his hands,
while she washes alizarin out of his brushes,
*madder*, until the water runs as clean as the paint rags
she hangs on the line, knowing that while he searches
in the rough for the one that's lost, he sees
his father's gaping eyes, horses stamping his hands.

## WAR OF ATTRITION

Left with one more axe to grind,
and no whetstone,
she went to his room and the small glass
where his teeth were sleeping.

She used them now and filed real slow
until the axe, honed and stropped,
was all steel gleam,
the teeth a millimetre short.

Returning them to their rightful place,
she walked out the gate,
the taste of a wet summer in the apples,
and he all talk, but no bite.

LAST MANGO IN TUBBERCURRY
*for Gerald Davis*

Driving through this grey north-western town
on a day of small things,
your hoarse brimming laughter
joins me from the car radio,

and I am back again at the Big House table
in that brief in-between time where our lives
touched off one another and you showed me
the different ways to eat a mango –

cut it lengthways to save the juice,
peel it like a banana,
or pulp it between my palms, the skin still on,
and suck out sap and flesh.

Then you brush-danced your way around the studio
to the rhythm of your namesake and Jarrett,
majestic in your robes,
as if the waters had just parted for you.

I stop to search the local shelves,
for one saucy, peppery fruit,
its flesh sweet as bees,
its seed sharp as tongue,

that I can rip, sip,
let drip down my chin,
turn this town to moving yellow,
a riot of carnival, turn this day.

ANY TALK OF EDEN MUST INCLUDE THE SERPENT

Everything so Martha's Vineyard,
so clapboard and white cedar shingle,
seen from the Island Queen that takes us
through morning fog to the first sighting
of the island's signs that forbid
motorboats their speed,

and Oak Bluffs with the oldest carousel,
all fairground horses and barker's jingle,
houses so wholly pink,
so sherbet lime and lemon sunshine,
beaming down on seasoned stores,
garden seats in the shape of butterflies,
fritillaries for the rich that, with a bit of luck,
we might even meet the Clintons on Music Street.

Talk of the monied and famous
includes those with their own osprey nests
– Pulitzers, Carly and Sweet Baby James –
hidden away from our yellow tour bus,
long stretches of shimmering green,
beaches to make films on, but

I saw a woman in the hardware store with a black eye,
though the door she walked into was gone,
and in Edgartown where the shingle
is stripped and painted each year
to keep it the white whaling town it always was,
I could stretch out my hand and touch Chappaquiddick.

## FUELLED

It's a day for burning down the house.
The wind incites the beast in the chimney
to lick its red tongue around the mounds
of stashed papers – books that inflamed your breath.
It will take the ice off the window you looked out of,
the wall you put between us, the door you left from.

Heat enough to make the dark uneasy
will drive the scorpions from cracks in the walls.
The black chitin of their selves
will scorch over the charred remains of your going,
and, afterwards, how cleansed everything will be
under the smoor of ashes.

# Of the Colour of Air, of the Moon and Seashells

'Things are older than letters', da Vinci said,
meaning that reflections on water and moon
were there long before language welcomed paper,
as in these pages here under glass
with measured air and light
that tell of the way his mind journeyed
from thought to tumbling thought,
unhampered by which hand he used,
the direction of its flow.

Recorded the workings of pistons and pile drivers;
how rivers when they rose in mountains
left behind the presence of shells
as the flood waters receded,
then coursed through the earth
in the way blood courses through veins.
He mirrored the possibilities of sun and moon.

That same moon drew me outside
to see its whole ghostly glimmer
between the horns of the new,
showing how everything has its shadow side,
and that sometimes it is better
not to see the whole picture,
better not to know that a dewdrop holds its centre
in a way the human mind cannot,
why storms at sea are at their most violent
when they are close to land.

ATTACHMENT
*for Evelyn*

Living as we do without broadband
the photo of you downloaded
byte by snail's pace byte. First
a pixel or two of hospice chair,

a line of stitching, before strands
of violet thread unwound,
a petal hinted at, grew to tulip,
stamen by brightening stamen.

Then your cap, its baby pinkness,
the frailty of your jaw,
your eyelid opening wide and clear,
the stained glass behind you becoming itself.

We sat out the thirty minutes it took
for the mauve rib of your cardigan to knit,
the startle of your fingernails holding
the clean outline of blueberry on cloth,

patient for you to network the broad
band of coloured threads to it.
Making us believe, for a short time,
that you were being born again.

## ALL DANCED OUT

She is tired of dancing for Degas:
all those pliés, arabesques, glissades,
arms held high for hours
until her fingers tingle numb.

Day after day she's on her toes
while he sculpts and moulds,
warning her to hold that pose
– the fourth position on the left foot –
but when she does, complains
that it's a poor turnout. So, bold as bronze,
she lifts her arms, pirouettes out of his glare
into a waiting frame.

Here the silken sheen welcomes her
to pillows in a scented bed.
A door opens and *le pédicure* comes
to hold her feet, her poor calloused feet.
He clips the ingrown nails, eases out the corns,
powders the milky skin between her toes,
his hand travelling up and up
until she becomes absinthe in his mouth.

## No Letting Go

Out beyond Stellwagen Bank
a humpback rose from the sea
carrying your child in its mouth,
the one you sent into the storm
the day shearwaters were blown off course,
you ran back into the house
put a chair to the knob of the door
prayed for the storm to go on,
and that she would arrive at the home
of a couple with more caring than God
who would take her into their hearth,
thank the storm for its gift.

But the whale placed her back at your feet,
waited to catch her first breath,
diatoms clung to her hair,
ambergris scented her skin.
She looked up at you:
*This child has come back,*
*the one you thought you let go,*
*the one you sent into the storm.*

## A Soft Day in Guernica

There is something about the way
the townspeople walk through the streets,
umbrellas up against the silent mist,

while we, our heads exposed, dodge spikes,
know nothing of sky or how things can
rain down from it without warning.

INVASION

The cicadas' first impulse,
when the ground warmed up,
was to unbury themselves.
After seventeen years, they moulted,

exploded into air. The fierce sound
of their mating pierced the everyday,
with weddings, Bar Mitzvahs,
Cape Cod barbecues cancelled.

Shielded by their coats, people
scuttled from homes and offices,
scared to get caught in the crossfire,
some afraid to venture out at all.

For three weeks they blocked out
the wing sound of buzzard,
loons sleeking across the canal,
the choke of cars on Sagamore Bridge,

while all along Cotuit, Clay Pond, Great Neck Road,
the females plundered the trees.
Their cutting jaws made slits in the bark
deep enough to favour future troops.

Foliage turning desert-brown,
the orange strip of their wings
on the small dark tank of their bodies,
as they took the town of Mashpee

where every flag fluttered at half-mast
for its warrior sons, toddlers the last time
these local invaders hatched out. Fiery eyes
now watched them come home in body bags.

HEROES

*A small bird will drop frozen from a bough*
*without ever having felt sorry for itself*

                      – D. H. Lawrence


I bow to the man who walks for two days
with small stones in his mouth
to keep his hunger at bay,

his wife who carries a goatskin of water
on her bare head, brings it back home
to wet the lips of each of her care,

or the woman who will not grieve
for her dead son in a neighbour's house,
because it brings bad luck, though

her own home is gone,
as are the walls of the school
in a village where no birds sing.

HEPHAESTUS

The sun was small fire compared to my smithy,
so I dropped the bellows and went outside
to see its last rays emblazon the olive trees,
the sheaf binders with their armfuls of corn,
before it sank beyond Mount Olympus.
In the weight of shadows along the path
a figure made her way towards me.
It was Thetis, mother of Achilles
who pleaded with me for her son on the eve of battle.
Born with my own mother's rejection still alight,
a lame god has few choices, so I brazed
for the hero all his mother asked.

Hidden away in my forge,
hammer on anvil, bellows on spark,
I beat from the small volcanoes of my ire:
a crested helmet fit for a hero's head,
a cuirass brighter than the blazing coals themselves,
and a pair of the finest greaves with ankle straps.
I cast a shield five layers thick, and, glazed with sweat,
chased on it earth, sky, a gibbous moon, two cities –
one with a wedding banquet in full bloom,
the other with a herd of straight-horned cattle
savaged by lions who cornered the bull,
tore him apart, lapped up his blood and guts.

When I had finished, I laid them before Thetis
who swooped on them in the way
a falcon grabs an unsuspecting bird.
Now, here is the myth: a mother thinks
she can protect her son. She will read his future
from the corner of her eye, try to call out to him,
but he must tear her armour from his chest
without a safeguard, walk into the flame.

## BAD RECEPTION

People say it's the hollow they live in,
built beneath the mountain, immovable,
but he goes home, even on days such as this
when the tight animal of his body
can scent the spoor of his getaway.
He slips his way through the door
to where she sits, curtained from the bright,
all picture and no sound.

He tilts a ladder to the roof,
his limbs low to the slates
on the climb to the aerial,
not knowing which part to adjust
so that it will deliver something
more than static from her eyes
that devour each little piece of him;
his going out with the lads, the odd
football game, the wood-turning class,
spalted beech curls in his hair.

He wavers at the apex of her salt silence
trying to balance what he's done, not done,
or what he should do to shield himself
from the scald of her blind mouth,
the smoke from the chimney.

# FOXWOMAN

Night and the covert of duvet about me
a skitter of shadow crosses the room.
With the stench of wet fur and viscera
she brings rain and her shivering body
into the space beside me, tells me

that to save herself she has been running
from those who feared the russet of her pelt,
who went gunning for her as she made her way
back to her cubs in their waiting,
a Light Sussex between her jaws.

The entrance to them earth-stopped,
the baying of dogs on the wind,
she hightailed it across stone walls,
brushed field and sink of bog
to arrive at streets that she slinked through.

The pelt of rain upon pavements,
she pulled coat tails around her face,
down alleyways where huddles
of rags and scats clawed at her
as she scavenged in the stink of bins.

She kept moving, making shadow of herself
by apartment hoardings, through housing estates,
up escarpments to open fields,
back to a cathedral of trees,
this open window.

She cries for the young ones gone from her,
guilt tears for leaving them alone.

I soothe her flaming fur until her mind pictures
their little snouts resting in dewclaws,
as if they had just entered sleep.

*Maybe it was their time to go*, I whisper
as she curves herself to my back.
*Maybe it is your time to live.*
My mouth fills with the aftertaste of blood,
between us the reek of vixen.

## The Past Delivers Itself

All of them holed up there for years
loose themselves upon the house
when the attic door is opened.
Down the stairs they clatter into our life
a hollow of bones on walk-about.

They thumb through the far side of yesterday,
reading birthday cards from one dead to another
or yellowed newslines of a troubled year ahead,
poke their noses into the brown cardboard suitcase
that packed itself with hunger across the Irish sea
and came back full of winter from Acton Town.

They wrap themselves up in the patchwork quilt
squared with the plain and purl of cast-off jumpers,
tweed skirts, coats, bits of blankets,
no fancy feathered star design or tumbling log
to hold small bodies in place at night, three to a bed.

One tries to make good the scraps of thatch and field,
of stone and smoke and cloud
that our mother shaped to make perfect landscapes,
while another twiddles with the old Pye wireless
tuning into *Mrs Dale's Diary*, *The Kennedys of Castleross*.
J. Ashton Freeman took me out of doors
to the certainty of birds:

how they called their boundaries into existence,
sang to ward off a fight,
or how their feathers twisted to let air through,
to flow over their hollow bones, so light
they lifted into the air, exalted.

## THE WIND'S EYE

Believing that she blew one way, but meant another,
he hurried out of his house to find the wind
and where she went at night
in the hope that she would dance with him.
He shadowed her into the mountain,
found the blustered reeds of sedge,
that hid nothing more than two lads
making poitín with their dog.
He breezed by a house on the cliff
where a woman brought him in her back door
and cursed him as he left from the front,
wishing him death in a fistful of rain.
He wintered in the eye of the lake,
until a squall soon routed the land
and carried him right to the quay
as the Gutters set out for fresh shoals

singing as they salted their catch,
then splayed like petals in barrels,
layer after silvery layer. There he fell in love
with one whose eye was full of gathering storm.
How simply he gave her
a pair of soft leather gloves,
three covered buttons on each side,
pink cashmere lining to soothe her scalded palms,
then brought her back to his house
where she stood at the door looking out,
and cried for fish scales on her nails,
the lye of salt lines in her veins.
Until the day when the tide drew the smell of herring in
and he went after a gust in the next town, she fled,
hanging the gloves on the barbed wire fence,
the wind's eye watching.

## Kai Leaving Gerda

What did I know of that word
written in mirror shards; its cruelty?
How splinters can be blown back into a person's heart
by too much of nothing to say at breakfast,
and more of it as we water the window boxes,
check the roses for blackspot.

At night I go behind my eyes
to where secrets are kept. Live it all again.
Does it matter that there was blackmail?
What I miss most is that hot shiver that rushed
through me as the Snow Queen beckoned,
sat me beside her in her carriage,
snowbees settling on the collar of my coat,
a rug around my knees.
Then she kissed me once, twice. Oh, the guilt of it.
Better if she had kissed me a third time,
left me for dead.

Let me just say this one last time,
you will always be hailed as the heroine,
the one who saved me
when you offered your red shoes to the river.
You let your breath take the shape of angels
and walked barefoot through frozen hallways
to spell out the word 'eternity' from slivers of glass
so you could bring me back to myself.

## THE UNION WORKHOUSE

The saddest note in this place is the colour
that falls through holes in the roof,
as do the birds, their feathers and droppings

thick along the rafters into the space
where a rickle of bones once walked
up and down between straw bundles.

The greening of voices echoes out of brick,
from ivy that grows in the windows,
hums itself into the corners of rooms,
playing the notes over and over.

A woman's hand stretches out just to know touch,
shoulders with blades, C sharp, that cut at will,
while the stars evicted from the sky
become ash blown from a dead fire.

Mercurial, the sky's dour spills from the mountain.
She has lingered too long in this place of the storm
that now roars towards her
and brings its flock of rainbirds
to peck and peck at her window panes.
It shocks trellis from its hold,
flips the cloche and drops it in a different place,
shatters the straight bole of oak.

She sees this uproar loosen the roots of her house,
this house she built on borrowed time.
It smashes the thermometer to the floor,
mercury spills out. She knows its element,
how with no walls to cleave to,
it breaks into a million quicksilver orbs,
that run in every direction, each meniscus
believing it's the moon in its own orbit.
Unbound, it cannot keep her winter out.

## HONEY-GUIDE BIRD

Consider
the bird
who holds onto
the needle-like barb
of its beak
only long enough

to pierce the shell
and kill the chick
who has just
perfected
its egg tooth
to peck a way out.

FLIGHT

His tread
on the stairs that small morning,
the rise of each foot,
the tock of the clock hid his going
out the door she heard close

of the home she spent her whole life
making, the one that couldn't contain
this son she struggled to hold,
who was never at home to himself.

How she searched for some sign of him
in the last of his words she upended,
any thread of him snagged on a bush,
nosy neighbours caught no shadow of him
on a road stitched with pockets of night.

In the dark that she entered, she prayed
to the ones who came back
for a glimpse of him somewhere
– on a scaffold maybe in Ipswich,
cadging fistfuls of porter in Harlesden,

even finishing a staircase in Mayfair,
his golden head burnished with shavings
after he measured the tread,
sanded the last line of nosing,
the rise of each going,
                    the flight.

## CACK-HANDED

When a left-over scrap of fabric falls
from the airing cupboard,
something about its selvage and frayed threads
lands me right back in sewing class
battling with a square of calico,
the making of a handkerchief.

I fold each edge into hem
as I have been charged to do,
measure out the elbow to fingertip
length of thread, moisten it on my lips.
With the silver spear between index and thumb
I pray that more than all the camels
in all the world, this white cotton
will march triumphant through its eye.

I anchor the first binding stitch to fabric,
and sweating fingers start to sew,
my stitch going in the wrong direction,
slanting away from what is right.
The hand chastised. A shame.

I am no Joan of Arc, a sword in my left,
ready to take the blame for the milk turned sour,
shield myself from the names spat at me,
gauche, sinister, cack-handed, to take on the flame.

## To Ground
*for Chris*

Thinking in verb: to plant, root, settle,
she moved to the place she married into,
five miles from her home, a granite coastline.
Spite in the wind that forced the few trees sideways,
little shelter from the things she tried to shelter from:
rigid jaw, hard mouth, a rock silence
when she hoped to chip an inch of talk
from one of them.

Nights after the house had fallen quiet
she followed the course of her longing,
back to that limestone softness;
the way it yielded to the rain
that let its own self dissolve into fields and rivers
rendering leaves of alder and hazel round.

It put nature on horses, built her people's bones,
as if they had drunk the very stone
from which they themselves had grown
and their faces, always their faces, soft, giving.

THEFT

The boy in the moon has grown to be a man.
He was banished by bad, dressed up as good,
for stealing a bush from a neighbour's field
that wasn't fit to fill a gap or kindle a fire,
and his only way home eaten by the birds.

The men who came and took one small step,
looked right through him, then went back,
left him with stars that passed him no time of night.
Clouds cover his face as he tries to look down
on the boy that he was who stood at the gable end

watching a happy fox knock apples from a tree,
or a sparrow on a wall in dread of the stoat
that skulked by in a jingle of beads
swinging its leather strap,
baskets of tiny shoes lined up at the gate.

If he dreams, it will be of a woman at her door
who smiles up at him from the linger of dusk.
She will find him a soft place to fall,
touch his cold lunar face, sing him back
his stolen years, one by precious one.

## SOMETIMES A WOMAN
*after Rilke*

Sometimes a woman
stands up from the dinner table
and walks out the half-open door.

She keeps on going, though
she doesn't know where,
and the road catches darkness

long before it falls.
Black thoughts she stills
with an urgency of stars.

## A TRICK OF THE LIGHT

Splicing together cine footage
from the sixties onto DVD,
my cousin presents me with my past.
This film holds everything:
breath of my mother, stretch of my sisters,
our brother young and at home.

The black of Mrs McGaugh's shawl
that hides her face from the lens,
milk churns in the back of the cart
where she sat me and wrapped me on days
when the walk from school was too long.

The squeal of a gate after Bomber Follen
dumped bonhams to rot
on that part of road where the tinkers
curved sticks for their camp.
When they dismantled it all to move on,
how I longed to be gone with them.

We standing around at Spiddal mart
with farmers spitting on palms
in the flicker and splice of the screen,
while cows watched me dig into sand
at the edge of the sea, so clear I can taste salt.

The frame of me smiling and something
of mischief in my eyes must be a trick of the light,
for I remember little that is kind from that time,
but a dark box of days, the barrel iced over,
a pinhole of bright in the night.

So much imagined, forgotten or never even known
comes down to me in these,
each one opening in the same formal way,
*I hope this letter finds you well, as its departure leaves me,*
learned no doubt on those rare days
when he chose school over poitín time in the bog,
his hair black as the hops in the still,
strong hands even then that went
to haul bricks onto lorries in Oxford Street.
Trudging home through the smog to a silent room
where he laid down words on the plumb lines
of blue Basildon Bond like rows of McAlpine blocks.

Penned to them all the promise of what he earned,
saved, wired each week to the west of Ireland;
decrying the days when he couldn't work
for the weather, or the pain, and how
the ganger sent him back to his digs
that gave him no light, no lock on the door,
and the rain coming in through the roof
for thirty-five shillings a week.

I follow his shadow down the scaffold of each page,
where he names what it felt to be held up against
the wall with a knife blade of loneliness at his throat,
and fight back with nothing
but the brown neck of a bottle;
hear his voice in the cadence of Mayo accent
that even on paper carries a surfeit of syllable
in the word *childeren* that he had too many of

and the promise of that registered envelope so clear
that to touch scrim still reminds me of the way it held
its grip on ten pounds until collected in the post office
on a Wednesday in ordinary time.
As God on the cross flew out of the sky
carrying His own blood from the smell of lonely
places, I read the loss in the hand
that ended each note with a crosshatching of kisses
no schoolmaster would ever allow.

## These Things my Mother Saw in Tea Leaves

Rats stealing the potatoes,
the black-headed cow in calf
the curving line of journey
the treasured luck of a fish.

She read them like her mother did
and her mother before that again,
taking the shallow white cup from the dresser
because a china white cup was best.

First she drained it clear of any tea,
we heard the hollow sound her hand created
as she cupped it over its rim
and clapped drawn leaves into prophesy.

Then holding tomorrow within her palm
she furled her fingers like a spring fern
into a curve towards her heart
and forespoke what was to come.

She saw Maloney's shed go up in flames,
the tip of a blade that pointed to false friends.
A tortoise at the china lip
spelled triumph after trouble.

When she was left with a notion of leaves
that augured his death, she waited up
night after night with that cup in her hand
for the guards to come to the door.

SOMETHING REACHED
*for Madeleine*

If hearing is the last of the senses to go,
as I stood in that telephone booth
in Playa del Inglés speaking to you one final time,
only a disembodied croak from cracked lips
travelled under ocean to the receiver in my hand.

Maybe what the hammer and anvil and stirrup heard,
other than the pump at your side clicking in and out
were: my broken words, the rattle of coins,
the man singing to himself as he laid out
loungers and umbrellas on the fresh raked sand

as your ear followed the waves
that came into shore, then out again,
it heard what they carried on their return.
An oval window opened to a voice
sweeter than your mother's, calling you.

NAMING THE HOUSES

I

This is what we do to retrieve half-lost, half-
forsaken pieces of ourselves, we go back
into places that are not looked for
until heard in stories that for so long
were just place-names that slipped off
our mother's tongue, as we took apart
the old range out on the grass
black-leaded it piece by piece.
We believed that every town in Mayo
began with the letter B:
Ballycroy Bangor Bunnahowen Belmullet
Barnatra Bohola Ballina
Blacksod Bellacorick Ballycastle Belderrig,
invoked for us again after a night of disconsolate rain
when a bog was riven from its hold.

It raged down the mountain side, its cold lava
boiling over houses, bridges, silage bales,
a wilderness of puiteach over Pollathomas.
Down over walls, a child's blue tractor,
swept half the graveyard clean away,
our grandmother's dust washed out to sea
as if her clay self knew to make room for one of us.

## II

In a cold season we five sisters,
carrying the raw death of a sixth,
fulfilled her wish to return to the place of her birth
and find the different houses where our family lived.
To see again the foam in the river which she thought
was from washerwomen upstream
scrubbing their dirty giobals on washboards,
soapsuds borne away in the curve of water,
bubbles arriving at her feet,
just as she believed the white droppings on the trees
were from some giant in the sky, who rinsed his
mouth, then spat it out after he washed his teeth.

We took the road from Galway
up through Tuam, Foxford, Ballina,
followed a sky relieved of cranes,
a dearth of white site notices flapping on gates
well before the turn for Glenamoy,
through bogland haunted by the ghosts of old trees
while the copper sedge, a monstrance of holy fire,
burned into the world of our past.

III

Seeds of rain dripped off sheep wire fences
and planted themselves in the sodden earth
beyond the door we looked out of. Feathers
of smoke rose from the one visible house in the valley.
Ruins of others, like rotted teeth, led us to the first
home our mother made, after she had closed the door
on an insistence of sandbags, sirens, curfew,
and in her high heels and London coat
took the boat back to her birthplace
to keep her then small family safe.
Our father sold up all they had and followed after.
They stayed a while in this rain house
given to them by a man from Boola
who had his own way of making potato pits,
small ones by the day, not big ones like the locals did.

Still the shadow of drills in the plot by the door
these walls mapped out in lichens,
*witches' butter* unctuous on trees
where our first two brothers played,
the black eyes of windows they looked out,
one of them long dead the other gone never to return.
Here for a time our mother used her canny ways
to stop winter dripping down picture frames,
pulled an unkindness of ravens from the chimney
before moving on, lorries loaded in the middle
of the night to his new job somewhere
across the border until the next one sent them packing,
back again to whatever house was offered.

IV

Here was our father's first place of knowing,
in the shelter of trees the home of his cousins.
All we could see: an old suitcase, its lid thrown open,
the shadow of bottles in corners,
the shadow of fire in soot,
the shadow of a small boy sharing a cousin's clothes,
his father dead, his mother living beyond Céide,
paid to talk other boys to sleep in beds above a shop.

We followed the road that drew him as a child
with his brother beyond the cliffs,
the broken nose of the headland to that shop
in Ballycastle where she served and waited for them,
in a home that wasn't hers, children not hers.
Instead we met the man she reared,
now grown to good old age in his own place.

This quiet man remembered how she was there
when he woke in the morning,
when he came running to her from school,
and there when his parents went to Lourdes in 1923,
gone for weeks, they were pilgrims across countries
searching out the mother of sorrow
– she was already serving shop and other lives,
dreaming of her own sons and, when,
if ever, she might see them.

V

Sometimes so little needed to travel back
down through avenues of gorse and rhododendron,
past a river that bore no foam,
no leaves un-spattered white,
roads that knew no traffic to find the husk of a house
where our eldest sister was born.
Just three walls left of this place called the forge.
Her recall of horses coming from all around,
the ferric smell and singe of iron on hoof.
These things in the earth we heard, half-heard
as we drove down side roads, turned along the cliffs,
to see waves break off the coast of this land.

A man in Belderrig checking lobster pots,
hooked names together like a net,
in no time got the breed of us, our seed,
each generation that carried music in the veins,
fiddlers in pubs, concertina players
making songs of what had gone before:
my great grandmother who came back
from the States during the Famine
to this land that had nothing but its own hunger.
She never again travelled beyond Belmullet on fair
day, where she went to sell milk, eggs and apples.
That money bought her a stretch of cloth
for a dress finer than anything ever seen in Holyoke.

VI

Sitting in the church that Sunday
we saw in the high cheekbone, the contour of jaw,
a tracery of connection to the people around us.
Proved we were from the same clay
as the ones our mother talked about
– the lost ones in the cemetery at Pollathomas
that the mountain had shifted that night;
remnants of its treachery still in walls silted up,
holes that showed where it brought
all it could with it into the sea.

We scoured the ground for names, found
Shevlin, Mullarkey, McDonald, Ginty …
nothing of our grandmother's,
but a fragment from another sister's memory
of the fire tongs pushed into the ground
by the far wall to mark the spot where she lay.

We searched all along its length trying to find
what linked us to that part of us gone.
No whit of identity, nothing at all to mark her leaving,
never to know if she were washed out to sea.
So I name her now,
Catherine Deane, our grandmother,
a woman with never a home to call her own,
her two boys separated from her,
one of them our father,
who, as a child, walked to see her
with bog cotton to soften the inside of his shoes.

## AFTER THOUGHTS OF STARS

Once while playing in the turned-over barrel
it rolled away with us still in it,
holes in its rusted shell let spectra through
and we fell headlong down the hill.

As we tumbled head over head over rear
we became travellers hurtling into space
holding onto nothing but dust-motes
that streamed into our battered capsule.

Out into the orbit of silence
into wispy filaments beyond time,
light years away from knowing
how stars came into being

or that when it came down to it
what were we but an afterthought of stars
clattering back to earth
at the bottom bar of a Ballindooley gate.

KEEPING THE HEAD

*Now Ireland has her madness and her weather still*
                                    – W.H Auden


God's bones must know no damp,
to let rain fall on us day in, day out;
rivers with collapsing banks,
stocks and shares tumbling
and parishes of rich men
up the creek without a helipad.

Time to take heart from St Gregory
who travelled from Aran to put *smacht*
on the people of Cleggan,
but all he got for his holy troubles
was the head cut off of him.

Never one to be stumped,
he picked the bloody thing up,
washed it in the well
and put it right back on again.
Took to the sea

knowing that feathers don't
make headlines when they fall
– not like the golden circle of today –
but the eagle always gets
the soft bird in the end.

# Mrs Monet Cleans the Lily Pond

She trawls her net across the green rash of weed,
he watching her from the window in such a frenzy
he will not lift a brush, a palette knife until she's done,
her dress flounced into her pantaloons,
a hat protecting her from the mad Giverny sun.

In the gather of slime, she sees picnics *plein air*
with Mrs Renoir, Mrs Pissarro, though they don't see
eye to eye on dress fabrics or ducks' livers;
Mrs Cezanne, a bit too dry for her taste,
though she has a soft reasoning at the dinner table
when tempers rise, a glass knocked over
spills its red stain upon the white damask.
Then a voice gravels from beyond.

Her net fills with the smell of rotting.
She dredges newts out of their philanderings,
a silt of caddis world, of wandering snail,
a leech puckers to the cold skin of her calf,
while all he sees are blooms full and pert as divas.

## THE BEATERS AT BALLYNAHINCH

They come in to where the fire is
and a lunch that they have earned
from hours shaking game
out of the undergrowth.

Faces slapped by weather
their beating hands hold pints of milk,
its creamy lip will talk them back to the strength
they spent among woodland withering.

At their own table, those
who know the pleasure of the shoot
balance pints of black, its creamy lip
gets tongues to boast about the morning's sport.

How they watched the hidden take to air
And, sighting up their aim,
their fire, notched up each fall
from a winter sky – the woodcock

with its rufous brown,
its needle bill and black of eye,
joined once more with the fowling piece
at a window view, to kill or die for.

In pursuit of something tasty with his tea,
from the camouflage of pocket a beater
pulls a packet of Mikado biscuits
to be shared among his kind, then passed

across to the hirers' table
who bag the sweetened catch.
The castle settles into the afternoon,
logs in the great fire fall.

## WORD-STITCHING

Still with the memory of matinee coats
that her mother knit, she started small:

> cast on three fish words
> purled a line of pure water
> slipped a blue autumn

and she had knit herself a haiku.

A villanelle was next
in the softest chenille

> although she worried how to shape such rhyme
> read every pattern in her mother's book
> ripped and unripped each minute of her time

until she had shaped the perfect piece.

> And there was so much demand
> for her sestina that she had to open a shop,
> a tiny room on the edge of the square
> where the chevrons on the pavement
> matched the patterns that she wove,
> repeating the same word stitches.

> Now her whole world was caught up in stitches,
> and to keep with the growing demand
> she bought the building next to the shop
> that reached out onto the square,
> so customers could drink tea on the pavement
> while they waited for lines that she wove.

A man came in once looking for a tanka top.
She thought the style was long out of fashion
but he said he would pay her good money for it, so

    she stayed up one holy night
    to add the extra two lines.

She did a roaring trade in metaphors:
scarves stitched with blackbirds on spring mornings,
their saffron beaks blinding,
crossover cardigans of women soothing
silkworms from thunder.
Gloves with coy murmurings
and grand randonnées.

'The Love Song of J. Alfred Prufrock'
caused her such disquiet,
with the women all coming and going,
that she cried when she came
to the purple patch at the end.

    She spun Rilke into silk.

With Billy Collins she had to change needles,
longer, slightly sharper to weave in the irony,

but with Frost she didn't know which road to take,
since there was one promise too many to keep,
so she went for something like a homecoming
in a Wendell-Berry stitch,
and that made all the difference.

## WHERE YOU MEET YOURSELF

There are days you can't remember who you are.
You spend hours looking for old pieces of yourself

behind the cushions of the sofa, the bathroom mirror,
the eye of the potato, that safe soft place

where you hid the purse of possibility,
but words slip away,

you empty out pockets full
of useless rhyme and incident.

You open your mouth and feathers fall out,
– primaries and coverts into the air –

Lifted up on the thermal of your breath,
they roost in the crown of your head

then take themselves out the window
and play puck with the plums in the high garden.

You try to follow them and meet yourself
coming back with a poem

that wants to give itself to you,
but your hands shake too much to grab onto it.

## THE POWER OF POETS

Ancient poets were mighty with their verse.
A house infested called the scribe to come
and rhyme away all rats, the nation's curse.

Rats just had to hear the pen traverse
the lines of metaphor on soft vellum
and fear the poet who'd slay them with his verse.

Before the ink was dry, rodents or worse
were gone, young and old banished from that home
by rhymes too powerful for them to curse.

Times have come again for poets to coerce
those vermin who have cost this land some
pain, to show us all the power of their verse.

Bring those to shame who bled the fiscal purse
with biros blazing reverse this bleak outcome,
write lines too powerful for them to curse.

Rise up slammers, rhymers, long or terse,
become what you always wanted to become.
Ancient poets had power with their verse
now rhyme away these rats, the nation's curse.

## MOTHER AND DAUGHTER TRIPTYCH

I
Reflection

Whatever way the light this evening bends,
when I look in the window of the train
I see my mother looking back at me.
Yesterday every time the phone rang,
I expected it was her telling me
she was already six years dead.

Old enough to be my grandmother,
we never did the mother-daughter thing,
no clothes swopping, secrets, best friends
– mothers are never best friends –
though we shared the same mote
we cast from each other's eye.

Nothing much said but I left as soon as
the brazen orange sins of the spindle tree
confessed themselves all along the path.
I often think the part of herself she feared most
was the part she saw in me.

Now I see how life falls from us in the end.
I measure the life that she weathered,
see her in my neck's shrivel and scrawn,
how I might call for her in the end.
I know if I turn from the window
I will be myself again. I keep.

II
This Life Cut Short

She was never more than a name to us,
our sister's life that was only
the same length outside as within,
a head too big for birthing, tore our mother apart.

Too small for all we wanted to contain,
we ran through trees to gather hazelnuts and berries
or haws when all else failed
to feed ourselves like wildish things.

The whistle of a blade of grass between our lips
went skimming across the bog,
made our mouths tingle,
though gave us breath enough for whispers.

Years later, just once our mother spoke of it,
when she came to visit me at last,
my own daughter, sitting *zazen*
on the floor between us.

She cried for a child of hers
who could not make it on her own.
*In a world where we fight to survive*, she said
a girl has to be able to hold her own head up.

III
Instar


Before your daughter gets to the stage
where she is the nothing between egg and bird,
take her to the edge of the mountain,
light a fire, daub her skin with charcoal,
feed her bitter berries, the milk of dandelion.
Teach her the lore of the fox,
the wisdom of weather. Wish for her:
a spare button for her jacket,
loose change in her purse,
the taste of moon on her tongue,
a lake to mirror her eyes,
St Jude when things seem hopeless,
St Anthony when she is lost,
St Cecilia when she needs to sing,
to keep her from missing
the sure heart rhythm of the womb.

## GIRL ON A BLUE BICYCLE

Whatever way it plays with dust particles
and scatters out its own wavelength,
this different sky so blue it is pure self.

The young girl must have taken
a ladder to it and drawn down
the colour the Greeks had no name for

into her eyes, her wrap-around skirt,
her bike, as she pedals by me,
the sun falling into her blonde hair.

I follow her down Calle Cielo, up Calle Luna,
the storks lording it over the town
above the lapis dome of the *iglesia*.

Arms that tied me to myself begin
to move out and up like a dancer.
My body unfolding to the music of heat

becomes different in this light
as it stretches up to hear someone
sing from an open window.

I gather in my waiting hands the given notes
while the girl on the blue bicycle is so far ahead
of me now she has become the eye of heaven.

## THE LONGING

Back to just the two of them again,
when the day comes wet they drive west with it
to follow the flood of waterfalls, flaunt of gorse,
lambs with newness raddled on their backs.
Everything between them said and no reprieve,
they are rescued by two young hitchhikers
burdened with rucksacks just outside Maam.
He reverses the car, puts their bags in the boot,
and all the way out he talks for Ireland,
as he pulls myths from the mist
that settles on an absence of arable,
a comma of smoke in a lonely valley,
in his element, pretending the car full of family.

His conversation drives them by the railway line,
iron long smelted, its ghost running alongside them
out by Benncorr, Bennbaun, Benbrack,
straight to the hostel door,
seeing them safe there
like he would his own children.
Before Kylemore he wants to turn back
bring them for something to eat,
maybe they're hungry? She says nothing,
remembering from somewhere how
the last thing on the young couple's mind
will be food, parents. How all they'll long for

will be to strip want from each other's skin
drink longing from each other's tongue
their clothes abandoned on the musty carpet,
while the giddy wildness of their limbs
among the sheets they get lost in,
will be like mountain goats with scant thought
of the steep incline ahead, the driving rain.

## SNOW ANGELS

If I were sky literate I would have read
the cold in the grey cloud
predicting snow on Máiméan
that would be with us before long.
It fell from the great bed of weather,
like the aftermath of a pillow fight,
settled on collars hurrying home from work,
in the secrets of stone walls.
Turned rusted gates to pictures.

For three days the village stopped,
cars stalled at the end of boreens;
main roads blocked, people took to walking.
We met on the way with time to talk,
while fieldfares glutted on windfalls.
Youngsters in scarves and gloves threw snowballs.
We became a Christmas card.

Our children lay on the whiteness of the far field,
stretched out their arms and legs.
Then, like a compass, they drew them
up and down the snow in an arc
and when they stood up had left
an imprint of heaven on the ground.
We could hear them singing
*Hosanna in Excelsis Deo.*

## LOOK, WE HAVE COME THIS FAR

There was little we packed for this journey:
a fox's promise, the blue of a heron's egg,
bed ends from a skip on Northbrook Road
so full of woodworm we had to throw them back.

Me riding backwards on the motorbike
as we went up through the Sally Gap,
the curve of the Dublin mountains
holding its place on my lap.

Winters when pipes burst and snow lay
indolent on path and rooftops,
we sat before a fierce fire, weaving baskets
while cane suppled in the basin beside us.

You asleep on the back seat of the bus,
I wishing you would wake,
so that you could see it too,
the sun burning up the fog at Delphi.

We didn't pack for the children
we gave each other,
one with the language of your bones,
the other with the thin of my skin.

My journey west with them, waiting for you
to someday follow on. When you did,
you had nothing but the shape of my horizon
on which to lay your head.

Look, how we've come the other side of children.
Today, as if there were no tomorrows left to us,
you calm me in the way clapped cymbals soothe
the swarming bees. Closer than breathing, we hold.

## SPRING

The way it comes in through the window
wakes me before it wakes itself.

All winter long I have left the curtains open
unwilling to heap night upon dark

or block out a possible inkling of stars.
I have been waiting for a change, a defining.

Something about this morning even though
little baskets of hail empty themselves in corners,

it cannot hide the fact as I hurry down the drive
to leave out my blue bag for recycling

and sky filters through a filigree of branches
that there is something about the light.

A fabric that I cannot name
but a sheer garment that wraps itself

around me, touching my skin
until the animal in me long asleep, wakes

like the birds who start to sing
– it all comes down to light.

## About the Author

A native of Galway, Geraldine Mills is a poet and short fiction writer. Her poetry collections, *Unearthing your Own* (2001) and *Toil the Dark Harvest* (2004) were published by Bradshaw Books, Cork.

Arlen House publishes her short fiction collections, *Lick of the Lizard* (2005) and *The Weight of Feathers* (2007) which are available internationally from Syracuse University Press, New York. *The Weight of Feathers* is taught on the Irish Contemporary Literature course at the University of Connecticut.

Winner of the millennium Hennessy/*Sunday Tribune* New Irish Writer Award, she was awarded an Arts Council Bursary in 2006 and a Patrick and Katherine Kavanagh Fellowship in 2007.

## Acknowledgements

The Patrick and Katherine Kavanagh Trust for awarding me a fellowship to complete this collection.
The Heinrich Böll Association and the Tyrone Guthrie Centre where some of these poems were written.
The Talking Stick writers' group, Saturday Peergroup workshop, Máire Bradshaw, Mary O'Malley, Dean Kelly and Charlotte Kelly.

Acknowledgements are due to the editors of the following where versions of these poems first appeared: *The Antigonish Review, Poetry Ireland Review, Ecotone, The SHOp, The Stinging Fly, The Recorder, Crannóg, Cúirt Annual*, Western Writers' Centre's Poetry Day 2008, *Razzamatz, Night Balancing, Captivating Brightness.*